D0829004

It's all about ...

WILD
WEATHER

KINGFISHER
NEW YORK

KINGFISHER
LONDON & NEW YORK

Copyright © Macmillan Publishers International Ltd 2016
Published in the United States by Kingfisher,
175 Fifth Ave., New York, NY 10010
Kingfisher is an imprint of Macmillan Children's Books, London
All rights reserved.

Distributed in the U.S. and Canada by Macmillan,
175 Fifth Ave., New York, NY 10010

Library of Congress Cataloging-in-Publication data
has been applied for.

Series editor: Sarah Snashall
Series design: Little Red Ant
Adapted from an original text by Anita Ganeri

ISBN 978-0-7534-7269-9

Kingfisher books are available for special promotions
and premiums. For details contact: Special Markets
Department, Macmillan, 175 Fifth Ave.,
New York, NY 10010.

For more information, please visit
www.kingfisherbooks.com

Printed in China

9 8 7 6 5 4 3 2 1

1TR/1115/WKT/UG/128MA

Picture credits
The Publisher would like to thank the following for permission to reproduce their material.
Top = t; Bottom = b; Center = c; Left = l; Right = r
Cover Shutterstock/Minerva Studio, Shutterstock/Denis Rozhnovsky; Back cover Shutterstock/
Gary Paul Lewis; Pages 4 Shutterstock/BlueOrange Studio; 5t Shutterstock/Sumet Boasin;
5b Shutterstock/photomatz; 6–7 Kingfisher Artbank; 7 Shutterstock/Francois Etienne du
Plessis; 8 Shutterstock/Steve Smith; 9 NASA; 9c Shutterstock/Stephen Meese;
10–11 Shutterstock/Bern Leitner Fotodesign; 11 Shutterstock/Nicram Sabod; 12–13 Kingfisher
Artbank; 13 Shutterstock/andreiuc88; 14 Shutterstock/Daniel Loretto; 15 Shutterstock/
Yuri4u80; 15t photolib.noaa.gov/Historic NWS Collection; 16–17 Shutterstock/EmiliaUngur;
17 Getty/Ed Darack; 18 Shutterstock/Jostein Hauge; 19 SPL/Pekka Parvianen;
20–21 Shutterstock/Yoann Combronde; 21t Shutterstock/Denis Burdin; 22 SPL/David Hay Jones;
23 Shutterstock/3Dsculptor; 23t SPL/NASA/JPL/Caltech; 24 Flickr/NASA/Jeff Schmaltz;
25 Shutterstock/Ververidis Vasilis; 26 Shutterstock/Valery Shanin; 26–27 Shutterstock/szefei;
27t Shutterstock/Stephane Bidouze; 27c Shutterstock/Bernhard Staehli; 27b Shutterstock/
Ensuper; 28 Shutterstock/Janelle Lugge; 29 Shutterstock/hessianmercenary; 29t SPL/Jim Reed
Photography; 32 Shutterstock/Bernhard Staehl.
Cards: Front tl Getty/Cultura Science/Jason Persoff Stormdoctor; tr Shutterstock/Lindsay
Basson; bl Shutterstock/Ioan Florin Cnejevici; br Shutterstock/Karnt Thassanphak;
Back tl Shutterstock/Sytillin Pavel; tr NASA; bl Shutterstock/Dennis van de Water;
br Shutterstock/OlgaLis.

Front cover: Lightning strikes over dark storm clouds.

CONTENTS

www.panmacmillan.com/audio/
WildWeather **or** goo.gl/kC05xj
Happy listening!

Too much weather

What is the weather like today?
Sunny or snowy? Windy or rainy?
Most types of weather can be fun,
but too much of any one kind of
weather can be a disaster.

The beach is fun on a sunny day, but too
much sun can cause drought or fires.

This farm vehicle is stuck in deep mud after bad weather.

For most of us, the weather affects the clothes we wear and whether we can play outside. But for people who work outdoors like farmers, fishermen, pilots, and sailors, dangerous weather can make it difficult to do their jobs.

Fishermen often work at sea in very bad weather.

A warm blanket

Earth is covered by a layer of air called the atmosphere. It stretches for hundreds of miles above Earth.

The weather happens in the lowest part of the atmosphere nearest Earth's surface.

The thin layer of atmosphere around Earth can be seen from space.

FACT ...

The atmosphere traps in warm air like a blanket. Earth would be much colder without its atmosphere.

Weather balloons collect information about temperature, wind speed, and air pressure.

satellite

space shuttle

aurora lights

shooting stars

weather balloon

airplane

weather layer

This picture shows what happens at different heights inside Earth's atmosphere.

The wind

When the sun heats air near the ground, the air floats upward. Cooler air flows in to take its place. This makes wind.

Cool air from the sea makes breezes and waves in the ocean.

When we measure the wind, we measure how fast the air is moving and in which direction it blows.

Anemometers measure the speed of the wind. Wind vanes measure the direction of the wind.

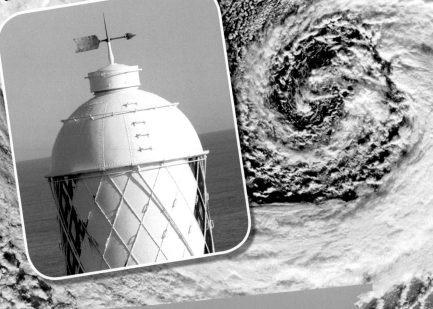

Clouds

Wispy white clouds and lumpy black clouds look very different, but they are both made from millions and millions of tiny water droplets or ice crystals.

When cumulus clouds turn gray you can expect rain.

Clouds come in all sorts of shapes and sizes. Different types of clouds bring different kinds of weather.

Cirrus clouds are wispy clouds high up in the sky. They show the weather might be changing.

Stratus clouds are flat layers of cloud that can bring snow if it is cold.

FACT ...

Lenticular clouds look like flying saucers.

a lenticular cloud

Rain and snow

Water is always moving around between the land, the water, and the air.

rain falls from the clouds

water soaks into the ground

When the water droplets or ice crystals in a cloud grow large enough, they fall to the ground as rain. Snow comes from ice crystals that reach the ground before they melt.

When rain freezes as it falls, trees become covered with ice.

water vapor cools and makes clouds

water evaporates from oceans, lakes, and rivers

rainwater runs into rivers and back to the ocean

Lightning strike

Lightning comes from giant storm clouds. Inside a storm cloud, the water droplets and pieces of ice crash into one another, making electricity.

When there is too much electricity for the cloud to hold, the electricity jumps to the ground as lightning.

FACT ...

Storm clouds can be 9 miles (15 kilometers) tall!

Lightning strikes the Eiffel Tower
in Paris, France in 1902.

Spotlight: Catatumbo, Venezuela

Record breaker:	most lightning strikes
Frequency:	160 nights per year
Rate per hour:	up to 280 strikes
Fact:	stopped January to April 2010

Terrible twisters

A tornado is a spinning funnel of air from a storm cloud. Tornadoes are also called twisters. As a tornado touches the ground, cars are thrown around like toys and houses are torn to pieces.

FACT...

Hundreds of tornadoes touch down every year in Tornado Alley, USA.

This boat was washed ashore by huge waves caused by a hurricane.

Sometimes, big groups of storm clouds near the equator turn into spinning storms called hurricanes, cyclones, or typhoons. Inside a hurricane are superstrong winds and heavy rain.

FACT ...

In 2010, hundreds of small fish fell on a town in Australia! The fish were probably sucked up from a river by a tornado.

Colors in the sky

When the sun's rays shines through raindrops, the light splits and makes a rainbow.

aurora borealis

FACT ...

An aurora is a natural light display seen in the far northern and far southern parts of Earth. The *aurora borealis*, or Northern Lights, is seen in Iceland, Norway, and other north European countries.

Sometimes, hot or cold layers of air form near the ground. They bend light in a strange way, making ships or buildings appear in the sky. It can make the ocean look like the land, or the land look like water. This is called a mirage.

In this photo the real island is in the background and the mirage is upside down below it. The lighthouse has disappeared in the mirage.

19

World weather records

In some places in the world extreme weather is fairly normal.

Hottest place: Libya: up to 136 °F (58 °C)
Coldest place: Antarctica: down to −128 °F (−89 °C)
Wettest place: Cherrapunji, India
Driest place: Atacama Desert, Chile

Only specially adapted plants and animals can survive in the Atacama Desert.

Antarctica is the coldest place on Earth.

SPOTLIGHT: Atacama Desert

Record breaker:	driest place on Earth
Average rainfall:	0.04 in. (1mm) a year
A dry history:	no rain for 400 years in parts
Terrain:	rocky desert and salt lakes

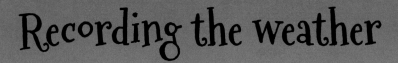

Recording the weather

Every day, scientists all over the world
measure the temperature of the air,
how much rain falls, the speed and
direction of the wind, how long
the sun shines for, and how
much cloud covers the sky.

A scientist downloads data
from a weather station.

The orange and pink parts of this map show the areas in the ocean with the highest winds.

Weather balloons carry measuring instruments into the atmosphere. Satellites take photographs of clouds from space. Radar can show where it is raining or windy.

a weather satellite high above Earth

Danger alert

Weather forecasters use the information from weather stations to predict how the weather will change. They look out for dangerous weather so that they can warn people.

a satellite picture of Hurricane Katrina

SPOTLIGHT: Hurricane Katrina

Date:	August 23–25, 2005
Highest wind speed:	174 mph (280km/h)
Category:	category 5 storm
Impact:	thousands of homes lost

In Australia, weather forecasters provide fire danger ratings during summer. Bushfires can start when it is hot, dry, and windy.

A helicopter drops water on a bushfire.

Weather patterns

There are four main types of climates around the world.

Polar: cold all year, with long, very cold winters
Temperate: four seasons, with a cool winter and a warm summer
Tropical: hot and wet all year round
Desert: hot and dry all year round

tropical climate

FACT...

Scientists believe that climates worldwide are changing because humans are burning too much coal and oil. This climate change is causing ice at the poles to melt.

Places in the world look different because they have different types of climates.

temperate climate

polar climate

desert climate

Survival!

Animals and plants are specially adapted for the climate that they live in. Humans have to adapt too—they need to wear the correct clothes to suit the local weather.

SPOTLIGHT: Thorny devil

Adaptation:	spikes on skin gather water
Lives:	central Australian deserts
Eats:	ants
Fact:	has a pretend head on its neck

This hole in the ground is a tornado shelter.

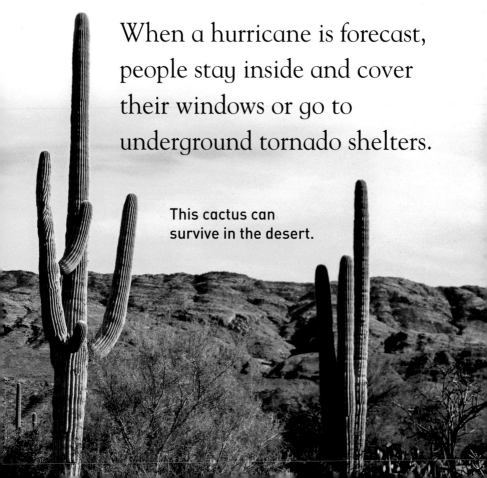

When a hurricane is forecast, people stay inside and cover their windows or go to underground tornado shelters.

This cactus can survive in the desert.

GLOSSARY

adapted Suited to the place it lives.

atmosphere The layer of air around Earth.

aurora Curtains of glowing lights that are seen in the skies in far northern and far southern places on Earth.

bushfire A fierce wild fire in Australia.

climate The normal weather in an area.

equator An imaginary line around the middle of Earth.

evaporate When liquid water turns into a gas called water vapor.

hurricane A big storm that brings strong winds and heavy rain.

ice crystal A very small piece of ice.

ice storm When rain falls through very cold air, becomes freezing rain, and covers everything in a layer of ice.

poles The places farthest north and farthest south on Earth.

radar A machine that shows where objects are in the far distance.

satellites Spacecraft that move around Earth in space.

temperature Tells you how hot or cold something is.

thunder A loud rumble made by a flash of lightning.

tornado A spinning funnel of air.

tornado shelter A hole in the ground where people go to be safe during a passing tornado.

water vapor Water when it has turned into a gas.

weather balloon A special balloon that carries weather equipment up into the atmosphere.

weather forecasters People who tell you what the weather will likely be in the future.

weather station A place where the weather is recorded.

INDEX